more recipes from
zarbo
a new zealand deli

more recipes from
zarbo
a new zealand deli

MARK McDONOUGH and ZARBO DELI & CAFE

Photographs by Donna North

A RANDOM HOUSE BOOK
published by
Random House New Zealand
18 Poland Road, Glenfield, Auckland,
New Zealand
www.randomhouse.co.nz

Auckland
New York
Toronto
London
Sydney
Johannesburg

First published 2003

ISBN 1 86941 581 7

Cover design: Thoughtfields
Photography: Donna North
Design: Thoughtfields & Random House NZ
Production: Smart Print Solutions, NZ
Printed: Bookbuilders, Hong Kong

www.zarbo.co.nz

National Library of New Zealand
Cataloguing-in-Publication Data

McDonough, Mark.
More recipes from Zarbo : a New Zealand
deli / Mark McDonough.
Includes index.
ISBN 1-86941-581-7
1. Zarbo Deli & Café. 2. Cookery. I. Zarbo
Deli & Café. II. Title.
641.5–dc 21

contents

preface

The thriving delis of New York, the bustling markets and culture of Italy and the South of France, the invigorating street stalls of Asia and North Africa: all provide me with food for thought and real inspiration for my 'shopping basket' to bring back home to Zarbo.

These are cultures in which a respect for food and its place in life is paramount, and I firmly believe we are beginning to see this same dedication to food back here in New Zealand. Yes, people expect our biggest cities to move with the times, but this food renaissance is blossoming in even the tiniest of provincial cafés. I'm constantly impressed by the wealth of boutique products grown and produced here. Innovative and infinitely adaptable, our young nation is becoming a culinary force to contend with.

Zarbo Deli and Cafe is a creative environment where the chefs are encouraged to experiment with ingredients and products and come up with new creations to enthuse our customers. I personally spend a good part of the year overseas, finding new ingredients and styles of cooking to bring home to an increasingly sophisticated and food-savvy market.

The Zarbo clientele (and now readers of my recipes) are passionate foodies; well read, well travelled and well educated. If an ingredient is available in New Zealand or they've read about something exotic in a glossy magazine, they expect Zarbo to stock it. So we do.

Following the enthusiastic reception of my first book, *zarbo: recipes from a new zealand deli*, I've worked along the same basic lines in this second collection, using fresh flavours and produce from New Zealand, enlivening, enlarging and overlaying these with ingredients and food styles from other countries.

I've been inspired by traditional cooking techniques found elsewhere in the world. There are some remarkable cross-cultural similarities and parallels. Asian Black Glutinous Rice Pudding has its traditional Anglo-Saxon counterpart, and seafood chowder, a real favourite in the West, also appears in Thailand and Malaysia, incorporating unique local flavours and adopting the name laksa.

I think most recipes already exist in a generic form, just waiting to be individualized by the chef of whatever culture. Some dishes though, like Spaghetti Bolognaise, or Crispy Vermicelli Noodles (traditional Vietnamese street food), are definitely classics, passed down from generation to generation. To alter them would be sacrilegious – these are masterpieces to borrow from rather than improve on.

In this second book I've also re-examined some under-appreciated ingredients of yesteryear. Quince, rabbit and figs all grow in abundance in New Zealand but are often overlooked or we've forgotten what to do with them. I've dusted them off and given them a new spin, which I hope inspires you to look at other old-fashioned staples in a new light.

With *more recipes from zarbo* I want to extend my philosophy that food should be a delight – easy to prepare, a feast for the eyes and pure enjoyment to eat. Keeping in mind how short of time we

all are these days, and the limited patience of hungry families, I've included simple, versatile finger food and selected dishes that generally don't take much time to prepare. Adapt, experiment, taste and enjoy. I hope you have as much fun using this book as I did putting it together.

Once again I'd like to thank Donna North for her unbeatable photography and food styling – my recipes would be but words on the page without her. Thanks also to Heather Gamble and Steve Barnett at Random House New Zealand for encouraging me in my fledgling book career; to Pat Field for her editorial help; to Helen Palmer who helped with the baking; to my sister Diane Dolan who's had less time to test recipes now that she's a full partner in the Zarbo business; to my Zarbo staff and customers for their ongoing enthusiasm and support; and to my wife Cushla and son Felix who are STILL there at the end of the day (even though, twelve months ago, I told Cushla to shoot me if I talked about writing another book!).

Mark McDonough
Zarbo Deli and Cafe
Auckland
2003

finger food &
entertaining

Finger food as a concept of eating is shared by many cultures, exemplified by the mezze platters served in Middle Eastern countries, boxes served in Japan, French hors d'oeuvres, Italian antipasti and English appetisers.

*a*t Zarbo, the brilliant platters put together by our chefs and deli staff often lead customers to ask how they can learn to do something similar. I suggest that it's best simply to experiment: buy ingredients you like or would like to try and plate them up; make items such as the Grissini Bread Sticks (p.14) or Baked Olives (p.21) to complement the platters. Think of them as a kind of picnic, fun or more formal, using fingers or forks.

Here in New Zealand we have an astonishing variety of ingredients available and we live in a real cultural and culinary melting pot. We can be hugely flexible in our approach to eating, mixing and matching and making up as we go along. The recipes in this section can be served as individual dishes, as light meals in themselves with some good bread and a simple green salad, or combined in platters that allow family and friends to select for themselves what and how much they want to eat. Some, like the Pepperoni al Forino (p.19) or Slow-roasted Tomatoes (p.21) can be made in bulk and kept on hand to toss through pasta for an impressive impromptu casual meal when unexpected guests drop by or when you've been at the beach all day and don't feel like 'cooking'.

Kelp Pepper

Used for centuries in the cuisines of many cultures, kelp pepper is now hand harvested in New Zealand. It contains a large number of minerals, vitamins and trace elements essential in a balanced diet.

Salmon, Kelp Pepper and Ricotta Mousse

Makes approximately 2 cups

Kelp pepper, a natural product of the sea, enhances the flavour of the salmon in this dish. The ricotta is a lighter, creamier substitute for the cream cheese that would be traditionally used in such a dish.

100 g smoked salmon
2 tablespoons kelp pepper
100 g ricotta cheese
juice of 1 lemon

Whizz the salmon in a food processor for a few moments until well blended. Add the kelp pepper, ricotta and lemon juice and blend through to form a smooth, mousse-like texture. Refrigerate for at least 2 hours.

Serve as a dip with crackers, spread on crostini or put into individual ramekins to serve as an entrée with a selection of crackers, vegetable crudités and Grissini Bread Sticks (p.14).

Salsa Verde

Makes 1-1½ cups

A classic Italian pesto, perfect to serve as a dip and especially good on pan-fried or barbecued fish. This recipe is somewhat more involved than a lot of recipes you might see for Salsa Verde because all the ingredients are very finely chopped rather than thrown into a blender and blitzed. The extra time is well worth it for the superior texture and flavour.

1 red capsicum, seeds and
   membranes removed, finely
   diced
1 large clove garlic, finely crushed
2 tablespoons pinenuts, toasted
   and chopped
1 stalk celery, finely diced
1 hard-boiled egg, finely diced
1 tablespoon capers, drained and
   diced
2 anchovy fillets, diced
handful fresh basil, roughly
   chopped
handful fresh parsley, roughly
   chopped
¼ cup olive oil

Combine all the ingredients for the salsa and fold through the olive oil.

Seared Tuna with Wasabi Mayonnaise and Salmon Roe

Makes 15

Try these when you want to impress guests – they really do have that 'wow' factor.

WASABI MAYONNAISE
2 egg yolks
salt and pepper
1/2 clove garlic, crushed
2 tablespoons wasabi paste
1 cup grapeseed oil

Place the egg yolks, salt and pepper, garlic and wasabi into a food processor and whizz. Very slowly pour in the grapeseed oil to form a paste (see notes p.118).

1 small loin of tuna
4 tablespoons black sesame seeds
1 cucumber approximately 15 cm in length, cut into rounds 1 cm thick
1/2 cup Wasabi Mayonnaise
2 tablespoons salmon roe

Cut the tuna into slices about the same size as the cucumber rounds. If the loin is large, cut it first into quarters lengthways, then slice these. Coat the edges of the tuna slices in black sesame seeds and lightly sear.

To assemble, place the tuna slices on the cucumber rounds, top with Wasabi Mayonnaise and 1/2 teaspoon salmon roe.

Grissini Bread Sticks

Makes 30-45 depending on
thickness

Grissini are served all over Italy.
On nearly every restaurant table
there is a bowl of them wrapped
in waxed paper. They can be
bought in supermarkets, but
making them is much more fun
and the final product is far
superior. 00 flour is a traditional
Italian flour, but plain flour can
be substituted.

15 g dried yeast
6 tablespoons lukewarm water
3 tablespoons 00 Italian
  (or plain) flour

2¹/₂ cups 00 Italian (or plain)
  flour
1 tablespoon sugar
1 tablespoon fresh sage leaves,
  finely chopped
2 tablespoons fresh rosemary,
  finely chopped
1 tablespoon chilli flakes
2 tablespoons grated parmesan
  cheese
2 tablespoons olive oil
salt and pepper
approximately ³/₄ cup water
a sprinkle of sea salt

Dissolve the yeast in the warm water, mix in 3 tablespoons of flour and
allow to stand, covered, in a draught-free place for about 30 minutes
until it starts to foam.

Combine the flour, sugar, sage, rosemary, chilli, parmesan, olive oil,
salt and pepper, add the yeast mix and water and knead with your
fingers until roughly combined. Remove from the bowl, place on a
clean floured work surface and knead for approximately 5 minutes
until smooth. Add more water if the dough is too dry, more flour if it
is too wet.

Transfer the bread dough to a large bowl, cover with a tea towel and
leave to stand in a draught-free place until it has doubled in size.
Depending upon humidity, this can take from 25 to 45 minutes.

Place the dough back onto the clean floured work surface and 'knock
down' to its original size. Divide the dough into 3 equal portions and
roll each into a sheet approximately 2-5 mm thick. With a sharp knife
cut into strips approximately 1 cm wide. Roll each one on the work
surface until they are evenly formed and around 18-20 cm long. Place
on an oiled baking tray, allowing space for them to expand while
cooking.

When they are all rolled and on the tray sprinkle with a little water and
sea salt. Bake in a preheated oven at 180°C for aproximately 10-12
minutes until golden brown.

Wontons

Makes approximately 24

Wontons are good fried, boiled or steamed, and are fun to make at home. Buy the wrappers from an Asian supermarket and serve the wontons with sweet chilli dipping sauce. Note, it is important that the chicken is thoroughly cooked.

FILLING
250 g chicken mince, precooked by frying for a minute or two in a little sesame oil
150 g finely diced prawns
a splash each of rice wine vinegar, light soy sauce, sesame oil
grated rind of 1 lime
2 tablespoons finely diced spring onion greens

Combine all ingredients.

24 wonton wrappers

TO MAKE THE WONTONS
Place wonton wrappers onto a board and spoon 1 fairly large teaspoon of the filling into the middle of each wrapper. One at a time, brush the edges of the wrappers with a little water. Pull the wrappers up to their points, forming a 'money bag', and press the edges together to secure.

TO FRY WONTONS
The easiest way to do this is to heat grapeseed oil in a wok, then fry the wontons in small batches until the pastry is golden brown and crisp. Remove and rest on absorbent paper towels.

TO BOIL OR STEAM WONTONS
Make the wontons as described above. Bring a large pot of seasoned water to the boil, poach the wontons in small batches for approximately 3 minutes. Instead of frying or boiling, you can also steam the wontons in a bamboo steamer (available from Asian supermarkets).

Excellent for cooking stir-fries, toasting spices and deep-frying, woks are inexpensive and if looked after well will last a lifetime — I've had mine for nearly 20 years. New ones need to be seasoned before using: scrub in hot soapy water and dry over heat (this is best done outside on the barbecue), then half-fill with cheap cooking oil and heat slowly until near boiling point. Allow to cool, discard the oil, slightly reheat the wok and wipe out with a paper kitchen towel.

Barbecued Chicken Skewers

Makes approximately 25

Skewers always look impressive and I like the exaggerated look of serving a cocktail-size kebab on a full-length skewer. Double this recipe to make larger kebabs to serve as a main. The Chinese sweetened vinegar provides a sharp fragrant note.

juice and grated rind of 1 lemon
2 tablespoons fish sauce
2 cloves garlic, finely chopped
2 tablespoons Chinese sweetened rice vinegar
salt and pepper
2 chicken breasts, finely ribboned into approximately 5-10 mm slices

Combine the lemon juice, rind, fish sauce, garlic, vinegar, salt and pepper and marinate the chicken for a minimum of 2 hours. (Use this time to soak the sticks in cold water to prevent them from burning when cooking.) Then thread onto satay sticks

Heat a grillplate until smoking point. Place the kebabs on the plate, cook in small batches a few minutes each side. Ensure that the chicken is thoroughly cooked before serving.

Pepperoni al Forino

Serves 6

Capsicums are thought to have been first introduced into Italy by the Spaniards when they conquered Sicily. I make this summer classic in bulk and store it in my fridge. It will keep 4-5 days and is a good standby to have on hand for when people drop around. Serve on grilled bruschetta, on an antipasto platter, or toss through pasta to make a simple meal.

1 onion, finely sliced
4 tablespoons olive oil
4 cloves garlic, crushed and finely sliced
1 small red chilli, deseeded and finely chopped (optional)
1 kg mixed red and orange capsicums, seeds and membranes removed, halved then cut into 1.5 cm strips
2 bay leaves
1 teaspoon chopped oregano
1 teaspoon chopped marjoram
1 sprig of rosemary, chopped
1 tablespoon balsamic vinegar
1 teaspoon sugar
1/2 cup dry white wine

Sauté the onion in the olive oil until translucent, add the garlic and sauté 1 minute.

Add all the other ingredients and mix well. Cook over a medium heat, stirring occasionally, until the capsicums are tender and the juice has evaporated, approximately 30-45 minutes.

Insalata Caprese

Makes 15-20

Insalata Caprese is a stunning traditional Italian salad. In this variation I have diced everything very finely to create a finger food. I've also used very small cocktail pastry cups which are available in specialty food stores and the deli section of leading supermarkets. If they are unavailable, try serving on crostini.

3 tomatoes, deseeded and finely diced
3 bocconcini, finely diced
1 large tablespoon torn basil leaves
salt and pepper

2 tablespoons extra virgin olive oil
1 tablespoon balsamic vinegar
1 very small clove garlic, very finely diced

Combine the tomato and bocconcini and drain off excess liquid. Add the basil, salt and pepper and combine well. It is important to tear the basil rather than chop it because chopped basil will discolour quickly.

Combine the oil, balsamic and garlic for dressing.

Place the tomato mixture into the pastry cases and just before serving, top with the dressing.

Note: This should be quite dry – if too much liquid is included the pastry will go soggy.

Slow-roasted Tomatoes

Serves 4-6

These are good to have on hand. Use either as an antipasto or toss through pasta with some rocket and parmesan to create a quick flavoursome salad. I have left the tomatoes whole on their vine but you can also cut them in half, which is more traditional.

2 trays vine-ripened tomatoes
2 cloves garlic, finely diced
2 teaspoons fresh rosemary, finely chopped
1/3 cup olive oil
1 tablespoon balsamic vinegar
sea salt and cracked black pepper

Place the tomatoes onto a baking tray (face up if you cut them in half). Mix all the other ingredients together and liberally brush over the tomatoes. Bake in a preheated oven at 120°C for 1-1 1/4 hours until they have caramelised.

Asian Spoons with Minted Sweet Chilli Duck

Enough for 12-15 spoons depending on the size of the duck

Asian spoons are an ideal way to present this type of finger food. The flavours here work well together and if duck is unavailable you can use chicken or pork.

the flesh of half a roasted duck (purchased from an Asian supermarket), finely diced
1/2 teaspoon Szechwan peppercorns, crushed
juice and grated rind of 1 lime
4 tablespoons sweet chilli sauce
4 tablespoons chopped fresh mint

Combine all ingredients, chill well and place in even portions in Asian spoons to serve.

Baked Olives

Makes approximately 1 1/2 cups

An intensely flavoured ancient Sicilian recipe, this dish will keep, refrigerated, for up to 2 weeks. Serve with an antipasto. Here the baked olives have been placed on blocks of feta cheese and served with a stack of savoury lavosh.

250 g plump black olives
4 tablespoons olive oil
6 cloves garlic
2 anchovies
2 tablespoons capers
2 bay leaves
1/2 cup dry white wine

Place the olives into a baking tray, toss with the oil, garlic, anchovies, capers and bay leaves. Add the wine and bake in a preheated oven at 160°C for approximately 30 minutes until the olives plump up.

Vietnamese Rice-paper Rolls

Serves 4

Vietnamese food is one of my favourites. It is a lot lighter and fresher in flavour than many other Asian cuisines. Rice-paper noodles are available in Asian stores and you can change the filling ingredients to suit your own taste. I have made this vegetarian, but chicken, duck, beef, fish or pork could be added.

8 sheets rice-paper noodles, cut in half
2 heads spinach, blanched and well drained
1 pack snow mushrooms
a few Chinese chives
1 carrot, finely julienned
1 red capsicum, seeds and membranes removed and finely sliced
Vietnamese mint
fresh coriander

The key to making these is to have all the ingredients ready so that when you come to assemble them you can work quite quickly. Make 1 roll at a time.

Soak the rice-paper noodle in warm water for approximately 30 seconds. Transfer onto a stainless steel or marble surface or a large flat plate (do not place on a wooden board as this will dry them out). Layer with the spinach, mushrooms, chives, carrot, capsicum, mint and coriander. Roll until tight, slightly wet the edge of the rice paper and press to seal.

As you make these, place them on a serving platter and cover with a lightweight damp cloth. Keep them covered until you are ready to serve.

Baba Ganoush

Makes 1¹/₂-2 cups

This traditional Middle Eastern dip is wonderful served as finger food with mini-pappadams. Serve it as a dip, or spoon a little onto each pappadam just before serving and garnish with a few chives.

1 large eggplant, peeled and diced
1 small onion, chopped
2 small red chillies, deseeded and chopped
2 cloves garlic
1 teaspoon brown sugar
2 tablespoons olive oil
¹/₂ teaspoon salt
¹/₂ teaspoon pepper

juice of 1 lemon
2 tablespoons tahini
1 teaspoon cumin

3 tablespoons fresh parsley, chopped

Mix the eggplant, onion, chillies, garlic, brown sugar, olive oil, salt and pepper, place on a baking tray and roast in a preheated oven at 160°C until soft, golden and caramelised, about 45 minutes.

Place all in a food processor with the lemon juice, tahini and cumin. Process until well combined. Stir through the parsley.

salads

A garnish, an accompaniment, a meal; salads are always good to eat
and usually good for your health. (Take note: many are covered with
very dense and high-fat dressings, delightfully rich but debatably
beneficial!) With a little flair, salads can be dinner-table decorations
in their own right.

Salads aren't new – some, like the Waldorf (p.33) and Caesar (used in the sandwich on p.47) have been around for years – but now that we're aware of how beneficial fruit and vegetables are for our bodies, and more familiar with the huge range of readily available Asian and other exotic ingredients, our concept and use of salads have expanded.

There are some basic considerations when making salads. The first is freshness of ingredients. The produce you use has to be at its peak, so buying and storing are important. It is never a clever economy to buy vegetables on 'special' that are about to wilt.

Salad components don't all need to be raw. Roasting and cooling ingredients such as capsicums and beetroot, intensifies their flavours and gives them subtle overtones, as well as a softer texture that contrasts interestingly and satisfyingly with more crunchy uncooked ingredients.

Colour and texture are almost as important as taste. The dark plumpness and light creaminess of black olives and feta, a spectrum of sunset-coloured vegetables set off by various cool greens, create a sensual experience quite apart from their flavour.

Finally, a salad can be a combination of whatever takes your fancy – innovate, experiment: add pasta or pulses to bulk out a salad into a meal; try various cheeses to give sharp notes; play with sweet and sour, soft and hard, traditional and totally unexpected. And try dressings such as the Asian Vinaigrette (p.122) or Wasabi Dressing (p.122) to transform the simplest greens.

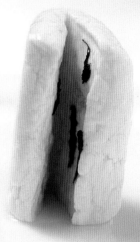

Halloumi Cheese

Now commonly available in New Zealand, Halloumi is a cheese native to Cyprus. It's made of a combination of cow, goat and sheep milk and layered with mint. It can be eaten as is, but I think it is best pan-fried.

Roasted Beetroot Salad with Roasted Capsicums, Cherry Tomatoes and Halloumi

Serves 6

Roasting the beetroot really intensifies their flavour. I love the colours of this salad; the reds of the beetroot, capsicums and tomatoes contrasting with the texture of the pale Halloumi.

1.25 kg beetroot, trimmed
1 red capsicum, seared, peeled and cut into ribbons
1 cup of cherry tomatoes, halved
200 g Halloumi cheese, sliced and panfried until lightly golden
fresh basil leaves to garnish

DRESSING
1 small clove garlic, crushed
salt and pepper
50 mls red wine vinegar
1/2 teaspoon fennel seeds, toasted and crushed in a mortar and pestle
100 mls olive oil

Place the beetroot in a deep baking tray. Sprinkle with a little olive oil and cover. Bake at 160°C until tender, approximately 1 hour. Cool, peel and slice into bite-size chunks. Combine the beetroot, capsicum and cherry tomatoes. Combine the ingredients for the dressing.
Top the salad with the Halloumi and pour over the dressing. Garnish with fresh basil leaves.

Midsummer Salad

Serves 6

This is a variation on the classic Greek salad. I love its fresh summer taste, enhanced with a very simple dressing.

6 yellow scallopini, cut into sixths
3 dill cucumbers, sliced
6 tomatoes, cut into sixths
1 red onion, finely sliced
2 handfuls baby spinach
a few olives (optional)
1 cup cubed feta
olive oil and sherry vinegar to dress

Coat the scallopini in a little olive oil and lightly chargrill. Allow to cool. Combine all the remaining vegetables, add the feta and toss.

Dress with a light sprinkling of olive oil and sherry vinegar.

Puy Lentil Salad with Roast Pumpkin and Feta

Serves 6

Puy lentils are a versatile ingredient that can be used in hot dishes as well as salads. The earthiness of their flavour means they go particularly well with red onions and pumpkin.

1 cup cooked puy lentils
1 cup baby tomatoes
2 cups roasted diced pumpkin
1 cup caramelised red onions
250 g diced feta
zest of 2 lemons
1 cup mixed fresh basil, mint and
   Italian parsley, chopped
salt and pepper
1 cup baby spinach or rocket
   leaves

DRESSING
1 clove garlic, crushed
1/3 cup olive oil
juice of 1 lemon
1/4 cup balsamic vinegar

Combine all the salad ingredients except the spinach or rocket leaves.

Make the dressing by combining all ingredients.

Fold the spinach or rocket leaves through the salad and toss with the dressing.

Waldorf Salad

Serves 6

The Waldorf Salad originated in the 1930s when a chef of the newly opened New York Waldorf Astoria hotel was making himself a quick meal, throwing this salad together from the ingredients that he had on hand. This reflects the fundamentals of how I cook – simple utilisation and adaptation. In this recipe I have used pear as well as apple, which gives a juicy sweet flavour and counteracted this with the lime juice, unsweetened yoghurt and the sumac.

3 crisp red-skinned apples, cored and finely sliced, lightly coated with lime juice
1 nashi pear, cored and finely sliced, lightly coated with lime juice
2 crisp celery stalks, finely sliced
1 cup snow peas, topped and tailed and cut in half
1/2 cup muscatels
1/4 cup shelled pistachio nuts

DRESSING
100 mls unsweetened yoghurt
1 tablespoon grated palm sugar
1/4 teaspoon sumac (available from specialty food stores)

Arrange the apple, pear, celery and snow peas on a serving platter, add half of the muscatels and pistachios.

Combine the ingredients for the dressing and fold through the salad. Top with the remaining pistachios and muscatels.

Variation: Use smoked paprika instead of the sumac.

KALAMATA OLIVES

South Indian Cottage Beans

Serves 6-8

This substantial salad is a meal in itself. It is based on a traditional recipe from Goa, where the combination of beans and cheese is common.

250 g turtle beans (available from wholefood stores, specialty food stores and major supermarkets)
250 g black-eyed beans
2 cups green beans, blanched
6 tomatoes, roughly chopped
1 medium-size red onion, halved and finely sliced
2 tablespoons shredded fresh ginger
6 cloves garlic, finely sliced
1 cup fresh mint, roughly chopped
1 small red chilli, finely sliced
salt and pepper
1 cup cottage cheese
a few coriander leaves, for garnish

Soak the turtle and black-eyed beans separately in cold water overnight (see notes on p.37), drain and rinse well. Cook separately in boiling salted water until tender, approximately 25 minutes.

Combine the green beans, tomatoes, onion, ginger, garlic, mint, chilli, salt, pepper and cottage cheese together. Fold the drained cooked beans (still warm) through the cheese and vegetables and garnish with the coriander.

Note: This can be served warm or left to rest for a few hours, in which time the flavours change quite dramatically.

Dried beans are high in protein and other minerals and are a staple of many cuisines, but neeed to be soaked before cooking. Rinse the beans, put them in a bowl, cover with plenty of cold water (they swell during soaking) and leave overnight. To cook, drain the water the beans have been soaked in, cover with fresh cold water to a level approximately 5 cm higher than the beans. Bring to the boil, reduce heat and simmer until the beans are tender.

Kumara, Coconut and Ginger Salad

Serves 6

This lovely tropical salad is ideally suited to serving with a summer barbecue. The richness of the coconut milk and sweetness of the mint are well balanced by the acidity of the lemon juice.

1 kg kumara, peeled, diced and cooked until tender, rinsed and cooled
2 red capsicums, seeds and membranes removed, sliced
150 g green beans, blanched and refreshed in iced water

DRESSING
125 g coconut milk
2 teaspoons shredded ginger
6 mint leaves, shredded
juice of 1 lemon
salt and pepper

Place the kumara, capsicum and green beans in a bowl. Combine the ingredients for the dressing, and pour over vegetables. Toss well, chill.

Bring up to room temperature before serving.

Asian Chicken Salad with Lime and Kelp Pepper Dressing

Serves 4 as a main or 6 as a side dish

For this very low-fat, high-protein salad you can use your favourite vegetables or whatever is in season. Vegans can omit the chicken.

2 chicken breasts, flattened and cut into quarters, marinated in the juice of 1 lemon and 2 teaspoons sesame oil

12 asparagus spears
1/2 head of broccoli, cut into small florets
2 handfuls green beans
1 carrot, julienned
1 red capsicum, seeds and membranes removed, sliced
1 firm block tofu, cubed
a few Asian chive stalks for garnishing

DRESSING
juice and grated rind of 1 lime
3 teaspoons kelp pepper
pinch of salt
20 mls fish sauce
20 mls kecap manis
100 mls mirin

Barbecue the chicken and set aside to cool. One at a time, blanch the asparagus, broccoli, green beans and carrot in boiling water until al dente. Assemble the salad, adding the capsicum and tofu.

Combine the dressing ingredients and mix well. Coat the salad ingredients with the dressing.

Garnish with Asian chive stalks.

light meals

In recent years we've been bombarded with food information —
cookbooks, magazines, TV programmes and newspaper features present
thousands of facts about food, scientific statistics and ideas about
eating. Out of all this has emerged a strong trend toward lighter meals,
to suit our casual lifestyle and to benefit our health.

*t*he light meals I've put together in this section are not so much invented as adapted, taking the best from many cultures, often overlaying or substituting flavours to provide a new twist to the taste. For example, the Gazpacho, a traditional peasant soup from Spain, has evolved as an Asian version (p.61). Using Japanese rice vinegar instead of coconut cream in a French Polynesian, rather rich, raw fish dish gives a simple, fresher character (Marinated Raw Snapper, p.61).

However, in many instances, traditional techniques and flavours developed over generations and centuries cannot be bettered; if you cook the Linguini with Clams, Lemon and Oregano (p.50), you'll be presenting an authentic dish that Italians on the Amalfi Coast perfected long ago and have been enjoying ever since. Basic methods of transforming simple ingredients into classic combinations are surprisingly similar across many different cultures.

So each time you try one of these recipes you will learn something of the art of cooking, as well as producing a memorable meal. If some of the Asian and other ingredients are not in your pantry, make the effort to find them, buy them, try them – acquaint yourself with their characteristics, see how they transform more familiar ingredients, and experiment with them when you're throwing together 'everyday' meals.

The dishes in this section are suitable for casual entertaining, light lunches, entrées . . . some will travel in a lunchbox, e.g. the Beef Wraps with Tomato Corn Salsa (p.59) and several would make delicious snacks as leftovers, such as the Smoked Fish and Watercress Tart (p.48).

Pasta

Good-quality Italian dried pasta (not necessarily expensive) is a pantry staple. Unlike local commercially manufactured brands, Italian pasta contains higher levels of semolina which doesn't absorb as much water and makes the pasta firmer when cooked, making it easier to achieve the perfect al dente texture. I find most supermarket available fresh pastas are not very good – however, freshly homemade pasta can be excellent.

Orecchiette with Peas and Blue Cheese

Serves 6 as an entrée, 4 as a main

Orecchiette are small pasta shells whose name translates into 'little ears'. This tasty dish is simple to prepare, but is very rich. I would suggest serving it as an entrée. You can replace the Gorgonzola with any creamy blue cheese.

1 medium onion, finely diced
150 g Gorgonzola, crumbled
2 cloves garlic, diced
1/2 cup cream
400 g orecchiette pasta, cooked according to packet instructions, drained
2 cups peas
1 cup snow peas, thinly sliced
2 tablespoons grated parmesan cheese

Sauté the onion in a little olive oil, add the blue cheese and garlic and stir in the cream to form a sauce. Add the cooked pasta, the peas and 2/3 of the snow peas. Stir until well combined and top with the remaining snow peas and parmesan.

Asian Green Stir-fry

Serves 6

One of the benefits of the changing face of New Zealand is the exciting food culture that is developing in our cities. I keep finding vegetables in my local Asian supermarket I've never seen before. In this recipe I have used a range of Asian vegetables and a Chinese sweetened vinegar, also readily available in these supermarkets. Note that some greens absorb more liquid than others, so it may be necessary to adjust the amount.

50 mls sesame oil
1 onion, finely sliced
2 cloves garlic, crushed
2 cm piece of ginger, finely julienned
1 red capsicum, sliced
1 carrot, julienned
6 snake beans, cut into 5 cm pieces
50 mls fish sauce
100 mls Chinese sweetened rice vinegar
juice of 2 lemons
4 good-size handfuls of assorted Asian greens, torn into pieces
handful of roughly chopped coriander
handful of bean sprouts
salt and pepper

Heat a wok and add the sesame oil. Quickly add the onion, garlic and ginger. Sauté. Add the capsicum, carrot and snake beans and sauté. Add the fish sauce, sweetened vinegar and lemon juice and reduce. Finally add the Asian greens, coriander and bean sprouts, season with salt and pepper.

Serve on noodles or steamed rice.

Salmon Caesar Sandwich

Serves 6-8

Sandwiches are an essential of any deli and are always popular. This one is a rendition of the classic Caesar Salad developed by Caesar Cardini, an Italian chef who owned a restaurant in Mexico. I've added freshly smoked salmon and used a long turkish bread that we sell at Zarbo. You may need to alter the volume of ingredients to suit the bread that you choose.

1 loaf Turkish bread or similar
1 head cos lettuce, trimmed and washed
3 tomatoes, sliced
3 hard-boiled eggs, sliced
500 g freshly smoked salmon
2 tablespoons capers
Caesar dressing (available in supermarkets, delis or specialty food stores) to coat

Open up the bread by slicing lengthways through from one side. Layer the cos lettuce, tomatoes, eggs, salmon and capers on half the bread. Pour over a little dressing to taste and fold the top back over.

Serve whole or sliced into individual sandwiches.

Smoked Fish and Watercress Tart

Serves 6

The slightly mustard flavour of this traditional and very under-utilised herb works well with the smokiness of the fish. When choosing the fish I would suggest quite a moist smoked fish, such as snapper, because it will flake more easily and will not dry out too much during the cooking process. Serve with a crisp green salad.

SHORTCRUST PASTRY

130 g plain flour
pinch salt
60 g butter, cut into small cubes
1 egg yolk
1-2 tablespoons cold water

Sift the flour and salt into a food processor, add the butter and whizz to form fine crumbs. Add the egg yolk and whizz, add 1 tablespoon of the water and whizz. If the mix is still crumbly, add more water. When it forms a single ball, remove, wrap in plastic wrap and refrigerate for 45 minutes.

Roll the pastry out on a floured surface, then place into a prepared 22 cm tin and blind bake (see notes p.127).

TART FILLING

1 small onion, finely diced and sautéed in a little olive oil until tender
35 g flour
3 tablespoons milk
salt and pepper
pinch of nutmeg
1/4 cup grated parmesan cheese
350 g smoked snapper
1 bunch watercress leaves, freshly picked, stalks removed
1 courgette, cut in half and finely sliced
3 eggs, lightly beaten

Sauté the onion, add the flour and stir until well combined. Add the milk and stir until the sauce starts to thicken. Season with salt and pepper and the nutmeg. Remove from the heat.

Sprinkle in half the parmesan cheese and combine. Add the smoked fish, watercress, courgette, eggs and the remaining parmesan, and combine. Pour into the prepared pastry case and bake in a preheated oven at 180°C for 25-30 minutes until golden brown.

Linguini with Clams, Lemon and Oregano

Serves 4

I can think of nothing more enjoyable than sitting in a beachside café in Positano, on Italy's Amalfi Coast, eating this pasta with a chilled glass of Pinot Grigio. This is a simple, stunning dish, and very quick to prepare.

approximately 48 clams (12 each more or less according to taste and depending on size)
250 g linguini, cooked and drained
4 tablespoons very good extra virgin olive oil
3 cloves garlic, diced
1/2 cup dry white wine
1/2 teaspoon dried oregano
juice of 1 lemon
2 tablespoons chopped fresh oregano
2 tablespoons chopped fresh Italian parsley
lemon wedges to serve

Soak the clams in cold water for 30 minutes before cooking and drain well – this will remove excess sand. Lightly scrub the outside of the shells. Clams do not have a beard as mussels have.

Cook the linguine according to the packet instructions, until al dente.

Heat the oil in a pan, add the clams, garlic, white wine and dried oregano. Finally, add the lemon juice. Cook until the sauce has reduced a little. Then add the fresh herbs to the clam mix and toss through the prepared pasta.

Serve with lemon wedges.

Fish and seafoods are plentiful in New Zealand. From the Rainbow Trout in our rivers to the many varieties of fish species in our seas and shellfish on our shores, we are spoiled for choice. Fish and seafood are enormously nutritious and I recommend that we eat them at least once or twice a week. The key is to develop a good relationship with a reputable fish supplier who is turning stock over on a daily basis, thus ensuring you're buying as fresh as possible.

Marinated Raw Snapper

Serves 4

In Tahiti I have eaten superb poisson cru with coconut cream adding a rich, velvety flavour and texture. Here I have taken out the coconut cream and added Japanese rice vinegar, keeping the flavours simple and fresh. This dish contains no added fat and is a perfect entrée for a casual summer dinner.

500 g snapper fillet
1/2 clove garlic, finely crushed
1 small red chilli, finely sliced
pinch of salt
juice of 1 lime
75 mls Japanese rice vinegar
10-12 cucumber ribbons (use your potato peeler for this or slice the cucumber very thinly)
2 tablespoons chopped fresh coriander
lime wedges to garnish

Slice the snapper very finely. Combine the garlic, chilli, salt, lime juice and vinegar and fold through the snapper.

Fold through the cucumber, then chill for 30 minutes before serving.

Garnish with the coriander and lime wedges.

Thai-style Wonton Soup

Serves 4

Wonton soup is a traditional Chinese soup. With the addition of the prawns and lemongrass it takes on more of a Thai character.

approximately 24 Wontons (see notes on p.16)

Make the wontons and set aside, uncooked, ready to poach in the soup. Cover with a lightweight damp towel.

SOUP

3 cm piece ginger, julienned
4 cm piece lemongrass, bashed and very finely sliced
6 kaffir lime leaves, very finely sliced
sesame oil for frying
1 litre chicken stock
3 spring onions, sliced diagonally
juice of 1 lemon
salt and pepper
12 tiger prawns, peeled but with their tails left on

Sauté the ginger, lemongrass and lime leaves in a little sesame oil. Add the stock and bring to the boil, add the onions, lemon juice and season with the salt and pepper. Add the prawns and the wontons and cook for approximately 3-5 minutes or until cooked through and hot.

Crispy Vermicelli Noodles

Serves 6

This is fun! Messy to eat, but worth it. I suggest you use the small bundles of noodles which are available in supermarkets; if these are not available use larger bundles, cutting them up with good kitchen scissors. This is a dry noodle dish so the ingredients need to be prepared in advance and the noodles cooked to order. The noodles cook in a split second, so keep your eye on them! The recipe is also good with cooked prawns or duck.

SALAD

the meat of half a barbecued
   chicken, shredded
4 spring onions, sliced
2 cm piece of fresh ginger, finely
   julienned
1 small carrot, finely julienned
1 cup snowpeas, julienned
1 cup bean sprouts
handful of mint leaves, sliced
handful of coriander leaves

Prepare all the salad ingredients and set aside in individual piles on a platter.

DRESSING

juice of 1 lemon
60 mls Japanese soy sauce
20 mls fish sauce
40 mls Japanese rice vinegar

Combine the dressing ingredients and place in a small bowl or jug alongside the vegetables.

500 mls grapeseed oil
6 bundles vermicelli noodles

Heat the oil in a wok and cook the noodles in small batches, turning once during cooking. (Remember they cook instantly – it is a good idea to have a trial run.) Place the cooked noodles on kitchen paper to drain.

Place the cooked noodles into individual serving bowls. Each person selects what they want from the salad, then pours on some dressing.

Roasted Red Capsicum, Chorizo and Smoked Paprika Soup

Serves 4

For a real taste of Spain, this is an easy-to-make and very flavoursome soup. It is ideal to serve as an entrée or as a hearty autumn lunch.

300 g chorizo sausage, sliced
1 onion, diced
4 cloves garlic
600 g gourmet potatoes, peeled and cut into quarters
6 red capsicums, seeds and membranes removed, charred, peeled and roughly sliced
2 teaspoons Spanish smoked paprika
2 bay leaves
6 sage leaves, finely sliced
5 cups beef stock
handful of roughly chopped Italian flatleaf parsley
1½ cups cooked long-grain rice (optional)
salt and pepper

Sauté the chorizo in a little olive oil for a few minutes until slightly browned. Pour off any excess fat that comes out of the sausage. Add the onion and garlic to the chorizo and sauté. Add the potato, capsicums, paprika, bay and sage leaves. Stir until well combined. Add the stock. Cook, covered, until the potato is cooked, approximately 20-25 minutes.

Remove half the potato and blend, return to the pot, add the parsley, rice, and season with the salt and pepper. Heat until the rice is heated through. Serve with a good crusty bread.

Pumpkin Gnocchi

Serves 6

Donna, who did the photography for this book, insisted I include this recipe as it is one of her favourites. Gnocchi are very simple to make and will take on any flavour you choose to put with them. Once you have mastered the basic technique, try replacing the pumpkin with well drained spinach or adding saffron to the potato.

250 g potatoes, diced
500 g dry pumpkin, diced
2 tablespoons butter

1 egg yolk
salt and pepper
1½ cups plain flour, sifted
2 tablespoons toasted pinenuts, chopped
2 tablespoons fresh thyme

Boil the potato and pumpkin until soft. Drain and press through a mouli or sieve. Return to the saucepan and add the butter. Cook, stirring, over a low heat until the mixture thickens.

Remove from the pan and stir through the rest of the ingredients to form a soft dough. Roll into balls the size of a walnut. Press with a fork to make an indentation on one side. Cook a few at a time in a saucepan of boiling water until they rise to the surface.

Top with a butter herb sauce or Basic Tomato Sauce (p.117).

Risotto alla Verde

Serves 8

Risottos are such an easy one-pot meal to put together. This is one that I often make at the change of seasons, adding asparagus in spring or green beans and green capsicum in autumn. As the name suggests, I have used only green vegetables. Experiment with your own personal favourites. Serve this as a meal in itself or as a side dish with lamb shanks or a casserole.

1 small onion, finely diced
1 clove garlic, pressed
2 cups arborio rice
1 cup dry white wine
approximately 500 mls good-
   quality vegetable stock
1 head broccoli, cut into small
   florets
1 green capsicum, seeds and
   membranes removed, cubed
1 courgette, cut in half and sliced
   into 5 mm pieces
1 cup green beans, trimmed
1 cup broad beans, shelled
1 cup peas
2 cups baby spinach
1/2 cup fresh basil leaves
juice of 1-2 lemons, to taste
salt and pepper
knob of butter
1/3 cup grated parmesan cheese

Sauté the onion and garlic in a little olive oil until tender. Add the rice and stir, coating well. Add the wine and deglaze, add 1 cup of the stock, stir. Add the broccoli, capsicum and more stock, stir. Add the courgette and the green beans. Keep adding the stock and stirring until all the liquid has been absorbed and the rice is al dente. Add extra stock or water if required.

Finally add the broad beans, peas, spinach, basil, lemon juice, salt and pepper, butter and parmesan, and fold through.

Beef Wraps with Tomato Corn Salsa

Makes 4

Wraps are ideal to serve as a light meal. Cover them in plastic wrap and put them into school lunches. I have given these an Asian flavour by adding black bean sauce.

600 g lean beef, thinly sliced
juice of 1 lemon
125 g black bean sauce

Marinate the beef in the lemon juice and black bean sauce. Cook in a wok in small batches and set aside.

SALSA
kernels from 1 corn cob
2 tomatoes, roughly diced
grated rind of 1 lime
3 spring onions, sliced
1/4 cup fresh basil leaves
3 tablespoons sweet chilli sauce

Combine the salsa ingredients and set aside.

4 wraps (or tortilla or naan),
available from specialty bread
section in supermarkets
a few green salad leaves

Place each wrap on a board, layer with the salad greens, then the beef and some of the salsa. Fold.

Garnish with a little extra salsa.

Spinach and Blue Cheese Torta

Serves 8

This is a real deli classic and so easy to cook at home. The crisp polenta crust contrasts nicely with the creamy texture of the rice. If you prefer, line the tin with breadcrumbs. Note, it is important to squeeze out as much liquid as possible from the spinach and ricotta, otherwise the mix will be too wet.

approximately 1/3 cup of polenta
3 eggs, lightly beaten
200 g drained ricotta
100 g crumbled blue cheese
1/2 cup grated parmesan cheese
1 onion, finely diced and sautéed
** in olive oil**
1/2 cup cream
pinch nutmeg
salt and pepper
300 g arborio rice, cooked and
** strained but not rinsed**
1 200 g pack frozen spinach, well
** drained**

Oil a 22 cm springform tin and coat with the polenta.

In a bowl combine the eggs, ricotta, blue cheese, parmesan, onion, cream, nutmeg and salt and pepper. Add the rice and spinach and combine. Pour into the prepared tin. Bake in a preheated oven at 175°C for approximately 35-40 minutes.

Blue Cheese

Blue cheese has a very distinctive flavour and smell but don't be put off by this because once cooked, the flavour is quite stunning. Use Gorgonzola in dishes such as Orecchiette with Peas and Blue Cheese (p.45). Or try a New Zealand blue in the Spinach and Blue Cheese Torta or on a cheese board with sundried pears.

Thai Mussel Laksa

Serves 4

When working on this dish I had in the back of my mind that I'd like to come up with an Asian version of the classic seafood chowder. As the dish evolved I realised that, in fact, it already existed in the form of laksa. Laksas originate from the Malay peninsula and come in many different forms. Make the paste in bulk and freeze; it's great to have on hand when time is short.

LAKSA PASTE
4 cloves garlic
2 cm piece ginger, peeled
6 spring onions
1 stalk lemongrass, bashed and sliced
1 red chilli
2 tablespoons fish sauce

Blend all these ingredients together in a food processor, adding enough water to form a paste.

BROTH
1 large onion, diced
2 tablespoons sesame oil
200 mls coconut cream
500 mls fish stock or water
4 kaffir lime leaves
2 kg fresh green-lipped mussels, cleaned and debearded

approximately 200 g dried egg noodles, cooked and drained
3 spring onions, finely sliced diagonally
1 cup bean sprouts
handful of fresh coriander leaves

Sauté the onion in the sesame oil, add the laksa paste and sauté until lightly toasted. Add the coconut cream, stock or water and kaffir lime leaves, simmer until boiling. Reduce the heat, add the mussels and cook until they open. Discard any that do not open. Remove the mussels. Add the noodles, spring onions, bean sprouts and coriander leaves to the broth. Season, and return the mussels.

Asian Gazpacho

Serves 6

In summer there is nothing like chilled soup. Gazpacho is a traditional Spanish peasant soup, given a new twist here with flavours of Asia. The soup needs to be made in advance and well chilled.

700 g tomatoes, deseeded and finely chopped
1 small cucumber, peeled, deseeded and finely chopped
1 yellow capsicum, deseeded and finely chopped
2 cloves garlic, diced
1 small red onion, very finely diced
6 kaffir lime leaves, very finely diced
$1/3$ cup chopped coriander leaves
a few mint leaves, chopped
50 mls Japanese rice vinegar
juice of 2 limes
2 cups tomato juice
salt and pepper
1 small red chilli, finely chopped (if desired)

Combine all the ingredients and chill for several hours before serving.

mains

This chapter builds on my philosphy that food is all about maximum flavour with minimum fuss. The variety of recipes here – traditional and modern – means there's something for everyone. Play around with the dishes and I'm sure they'll become firm family favourites.

*t*his selection of dishes is derived from a broad base of major world cuisines. There are classics that should be left as such, for example the Mellenzane Parmigiana (p.69) and Spaghetti Bolognese (p.80). In other dishes flavours are borrowed and swapped, improvised and inspired, all in keeping with the current culinary climate of interweaving cultures and the avalanche of exotic ingredients available.

A Kiwi summer barbecued snapper is accompanied by an unexpectedly delectable selection of Asian sauces (p.72). Rabbit makes a comeback (p.75).

Impress your friends by serving them up the Seared Tuna Loin (p.81). The Chinese Barbecued Pork Ribs (p.68) will be a big hit with your kids, but make sure you're armed with plenty of paper towels for sticky fingers.

There are winter entertaining dishes that cry out for a fire, candelight and rain on the roof, e.g. the Moroccan Lamb Shanks (p.67), or North African Chicken Tagine (p.74) and vegetarian dishes that will delight the most die-hard meat-eaters (try them with the Pumpkin, Kumara and Tamarind Curry, p.76).

Obviously when you think dinners you think mains, but these dishes can also be lunches, supper after a movie, a winter brunch – the Winter Vegetables with Chicken Thighs and Balsamic Oregano Dressing (p.78) would be perfect for this.

Moroccan Lamb Shanks

Serves 4-6

Lamb shanks are always a favourite. They are really simple to prepare and if cooked slowly will be succulent and tender. Ras el-hanout is a traditional Moroccan spice which we sell at Zarbo as Moroccan Rub.

6 lamb shanks
3 tablespoons ras el-hanout

2 large onions, roughly diced
1 head garlic, cloves crushed, peeled and left whole
2 teaspoons extra ras el-hanout

2 400 g tins whole peeled Italian tomatoes
3 cups beef stock
1 cup red wine
1-2 teaspoons harissa paste (to taste)

Place the lamb shanks in a plastic bag and add the 3 tablespoons of ras el-hanout. Coat well and leave overnight.

The shanks need to be seared to seal in the flavours. Do this on the barbecue or heat a little oil in a pan and sear. Place the seared shanks in a large ovenproof dish.

In a saucepan sauté the onion in a little olive oil, add the garlic, 2 teaspoons of ras el-hanout, the tomatoes, stock, wine and harissa. Heat and pour over the shanks. Cover and bake in a preheated oven at 160°C for 1 1/2 hours. Remove cover and bake a further 30 minutes, turning the shanks a couple of times.

Remove the cooked shanks and keep warm. Transfer the liquid to a saucepan, bring to the boil and reduce. Serve the shanks and sauce on couscous, rice or with roasted potatoes.

Chinese Barbecued Pork Ribs

Serves 4

Ribs are one of those classic dishes I feel should make a return. They are so easy to prepare and so much fun to eat. In the States, ribs are big business and some restaurants are dedicated exclusively to them. Hoisin sauce (available in Asian stores and many mainstream supermarkets) is a thick, sweet and spicy sauce which gives this dish a nice richness.

²/₃ cup hoisin sauce
²/₃ cup light soy sauce
2 tablespoons brown sugar

1.5-2 kg pork ribs (ask your butcher to leave these whole)

Combine the first 3 ingredients and heat in a saucepan to dissolve the sugar.

Coat the ribs in the sauce and cook under a hot grill until well caramelised. This takes approximately 30-40 minutes. Turn the ribs regularly and reglaze them during cooking. Just before serving, slice the ribs by running a knife through the fleshy part between the bones.

Mellenzane Parmigiana

Serves 6

This is one of my all-time favourites. It screams the essence of traditional Italian cusine. The dish can be made in a lasagne style or individual serves, as I have done here.

2 large eggplants, cut into 18 rings approximately 1 cm thick, salted, drained, oiled and lightly chargrilled
1 medium onion, diced
1 small clove garlic, crushed
1 400 g tin of Italian whole peeled tomatoes, hand crushed
small handful roughly chopped Italian parsley and basil
salt and pepper
1/3 cup extra torn fresh basil leaves
200 g fresh mozzarella cheese, thinly sliced
1/2 cup freshly grated parmesan cheese

Organise the grilled eggplant into 6 bundles, each of 3 rings of similar size.

Sauté the onion and garlic. Add the tomatoes, herbs, salt and pepper. Cook over a medium heat until fully reduced and the juice has evaporated.

On a baking tray place 1 eggplant ring from each bundle. Spoon over a little of the sauce, top with basil leaves and a slice of the mozzarella. Repeat. Add the last layer of eggplant and top with parmesan.

Bake in a preheated oven at 160°C for approximately 25-30 minutes.

Filo Strudel with Salmon and Roasted Vegetables

Serves 6

We are all familiar with filo pastry ('phyllo' is the Greek word for leaf), but I like to treat it differently by brushing the pastry with a light olive oil rather than the traditional butter. The oil is not as dominant a flavour as butter can be. Adapt this recipe using your favourite chargrilled vegetables.

250 g fresh salmon, boned
1/2 cup water
1/2 cup dry white wine
1 bay leaf
2 slices lemon
freshly cracked pepper

6 sheets filo pastry
olive oil for brushing
a few spinach leaves
2 red capsicums, seeds and membranes removed, chargrilled and skins removed
2 courgettes, thinly sliced and lightly chargrilled
2 teaspoons fresh dill
salt and pepper
1/2 cup cottage cheese, well drained

Place the salmon in a pan, cover with water, add the wine, bay leaf, lemon and pepper. Bring to the boil, reduce the heat and simmer for 5-7 minutes. Remove the salmon from the pan and allow to cool. Once cool, flake the salmon.

Place 1 sheet of filo on a board and brush with oil, add another and oil, continue until all the sheets are used. Do not brush the last sheet. Leaving the top quarter of the layered filo uncovered, place the spinach leaves evenly over three-quarters of the filo, next layer the charred capsicums and the courgettes. Mix the dill and the salt and pepper into the cottage cheese. Spoon this mix onto the middle of the prepared vegetables. Place the salmon on top of the cottage cheese mix. Roll the filo into a sausage, starting from the filling end.

Place the roll on a baking tray, brush with oil and bake in a preheated oven at 160°C for 20-25 minutes until golden brown.

Serve with Dill and Citrus Aioli (p.118).

Barbecued Whole Snapper with 3 Asian Sauces

Serves 4-6

Nothing compares to a freshly caught (or in this case bought) whole snapper. The whole idea conjures up lazy summer days at the beach. It's also perfect for a casual barbecue with friends. I like to serve it with these 3 sauces.

1 whole snapper, gutted, scaled and well washed (if you buy a whole snapper from a fish shop they will do this for you)
1/2 lemon, finely sliced
small handful fresh coriander

Place the lemon and coriander into the cavity of the fish and cook. The snapper can be barbecued, grilled or baked in the oven.

Serve on a platter on a bed of Asian greens with the sauces to the side.

WASABI MAYONNAISE
See recipe and method on p.13.

VIETNAMESE NUOC CHAM
1 red chilli, finely sliced
juice of 3 limes
1/4 cup fish sauce
3 tablespoons grated palm sugar
1 tablespoon minced garlic

Combine all ingredients and leave to stand 1 hour before serving.

BASIL SHRIMP SAUCE
10 g shrimp paste (available under various names from Asian supermarkets; very smelly, but worth it for the flavour)
4 cloves garlic
1/2 cup packed basil leaves
1 cup grapeseed oil

Blend all together.

Think of your barbecue as part of your kitchen, not just an entertaining way to cook sausages on summer evenings. I use mine for smoky jobs like charring peppers, grilling eggplant and searing meat and fish. As an alternative, grillplates are ideal for indoor use: chargrilling vegetables and meat if you're wanting to replicate that restaurant seared look. And because the food is not cooking in a puddle of oil, grilling is a healthy, low-fat way to cook.

North African Chicken Tagine

Serves 4

Tagines are a wonderful winter one-pot dish. The aromatic flavours of this version will impress your family or dinner guests. A tagine is traditionally made with lamb, but I have used chicken to create a lighter taste. Serve with roasted potatoes, couscous or rice.

1 onion, finely diced
6 cloves garlic, bashed, peeled but left whole

3 large chicken breasts, cut into quarters
1 teaspoon cumin seeds, lightly toasted and crushed
1/2 teaspoon cardamom seeds, lightly toasted and crushed
2 cinnamon sticks
2 bay leaves
2 teaspoons dried oregano
1 teaspoon ground turmeric
1 pickled lemon, rinsed and finely sliced (use only the skin)
1/2 cup olives
8 Medjool dates
8 sun-dried nectarines
1 cup dry white wine
2 handfuls fresh green beans
handful fresh chopped coriander

Heat a little oil in a heavy-based pan. Add the onion and garlic and sauté. Add the chicken and cook until well browned. Add the crushed seeds, cinnamon, bay leaves, oregano, turmeric, lemon and olives. Sauté until the chicken is well coated. Add the dates, nectarines and wine.

Cook, covered, for 40 minutes to 1 hour, stirring occasionally. Add the green beans and cook for a further 15 minutes. Fold through the coriander just before serving.

Rabbit and Black Olive Casserole

Serves 4-6

Whenever I talk about cooking rabbit it creates debate. Some people remember their childhood pets, others remember those pests on their farms. The ancient Romans commonly used rabbit or hare as a festive dish, stuffed and baked or braised with a surprising array of herbs and spices such as lovage, fennel, cumin, oregano, chives and coriander. If you are using freshly shot rabbit, the pellets should be carefully removed.

olive oil for frying
1 rabbit, jointed into 6 pieces

1 head garlic, crushed and peeled
1 onion, finely diced
1/2 cup red wine
1 400 g tin whole peeled Italian
 tomatoes, crushed
2 tablespoons tomato paste
1 cup black olives
3 tablespoons balsamic vinegar
1 tablespoon brown sugar
freshly chopped sage, rosemary
 and marjoram
2 stalks celery, thinly sliced
1 carrot, peeled and diced

Heat some olive oil in a heavy casserole. Dust the rabbit portions with a little flour and fry in the oil until well browned, doing a few at a time. Remove from the pan. Add the garlic and onion to the pan, sauté, then deglaze with the red wine. Add the tomatoes, tomato paste, olives, balsamic vinegar, sugar, herbs, celery and carrot. Combine well and add the rabbit portions.

Cook, well covered, in a preheated oven at 180°C for 1-1 1/2 hours until tender. Turn a couple of times during the cooking process. Serve with roasted garlic, rosemary potatoes or with polenta

Pumpkin, Kumara and Tamarind Curry

Serves 4

You may have seen blocks of tamarind in a supermarket and wondered what to do with them. Tamarind has a fragrant citrus flavour that works well with the sweetness of pumpkin and kumara. As with all curries, I think this one should be made a day in advance, chilled in the fridge overnight and reheated before serving – doing this really intensifies the flavour.

$1/2$ block tamarind

2 tablespoons cumin seeds
$1/2$ teaspoon nutmeg
$1/2$ teaspoon cardamom seeds
$1/2$ teaspoon fenugreek seeds
$1/2$ teaspoon coriander seeds
1 teaspoon black peppercorns

1 onion, diced
1 head garlic, crushed, peeled and roughly diced
1-2 birds-eye chillies (to taste), cut in half, deseeded and chopped
$1/2$ pumpkin (skin on) approximately 600 g, chopped in bite-sized pieces
600 g kumara (skin on), chopped in bite-sized pieces
1 teaspoon turmeric
2 cups stock
2 tablespoons brown sugar
handful fresh coriander, chopped

Soak the tamarind in 3 cups of hot water for 20-25 minutes and strain through a sieve, reserving $1/2$-1 cup of the liquid.

Toast the cumin seeds, nutmeg, cardamom seeds, fenugreek seeds, coriander seeds and peppercorns and crush them in a mortar and pestle.

Sauté the onion in a little olive oil, add the crushed spices, garlic and chilli. Add the $1/2$ cup of tamarind water to deglaze the pan. Add the pumpkin and kumara, tamarind pulp, turmeric, stock and sugar.

Cook over a medium heat for approximately 25-30 minutes until the vegetables are tender. Fold through the coriander.

Variation: Add your favourite firm-fleshed white fish.

Winter Vegetables with Chicken Thighs and Balsamic Oregano Dressing

Serves 4

This is just one of those easy-to-prepare meals which is ideal for any season. Here I've roasted winter vegetables, but try it out at other times of the year with different vegetables, or slice the chicken and toss through salad greens.

4 boneless chicken thighs, trimmed of excess fat and marinated in a little olive oil, lemon juice and a few capers

approximately 750 g pumpkin, sliced

2 red capsicums, cut into quarters and deseeded

2 red onions, peeled and cut into quarters

a few cloves of garlic

1 small eggplant, diced

other seasonal vegetables to taste

olive oil for frying

DRESSING

1 tablespoon olive oil

40 mls balsamic vinegar

1 tablespoon chopped fresh oregano

1 clove garlic, finely crushed

salt and pepper

Grill the chicken on a hot grillplate or barbecue, set aside.

Prepare the pumpkin, capsicums, onions and garlic, coat with a little olive oil, season with salt and pepper. Roast in a preheated oven at 180°C, tossing a few times.

Fry the eggplant in olive oil and combine with the other vegetables.

Combine the dressing ingredients.

Combine the warm roasted vegetables, pouring the dressing over both the chicken thighs and vegetables.

Spaghetti Bolognese

Serves 4

This is the easiest of meals to prepare, a classic which if well made will satisfy the whole family. Use the leanest beef mince available and make sure that the mince is fully cooked through and broken up before adding the liquid. Remember this is served as a dry sauce.

1 large onion, finely diced
2 tablespoons olive oil
500 g lean beef mince
4 cloves garlic, crushed and roughly chopped
1 400 g tin whole peeled Italian tomatoes, hand crushed
2 tablespoons tomato paste
1 cup dry white wine
2 bay leaves
2 courgettes, diced
handful roughly chopped fresh herbs

250 g spaghetti, cooked according to the packet instructions and drained
freshly shaved parmesan cheese

Sauté the onion in the olive oil until translucent, add the beef mince and stir with a wooden spoon, making sure that the meat is thoroughly broken up. This will ensure the sauce will not be full of lumps of meat and any fat in the mince will cook out and evaporate.

Add the garlic, tomatoes, tomato paste, white wine and the bay leaves. Stir thoroughly. Allow to simmer on a medium heat for 15 minutes, then add the courgettes and the fresh herbs. Stir, and cook for a further 10 minutes.

Serve on the spaghetti and top with some parmesan.

Seared Tuna Loin on Somen Noodle Cakes with Salsa Verde

Serves 4

This dish shows fusion cuisine at its best. Tuna, which is a staple of many cuisines, is served on Japanese noodles and topped with an Italian Salsa.

4 tuna steaks
a little olive oil
salt and pepper

Lightly coat the tuna with olive oil and season with salt and pepper. Heat a grillplate to smoking point and sear the tuna for a few minutes on each side. Increase the cooking time if you like it more well done.

Serve the steaks on noodle cakes with Salsa Verde (p.12).

NOODLE CAKES
It is important to use Somen noodles for these as other types of noodle will not cook as desired.

1 400 g packet Somen noodles (available from Asian supermarkets)

Cook the noodles according to the packet instructions, rinse and drain well. Spray a muffin pan with baking spray. Place noodles in the muffin cups to halfway level, then spray the top of the noodles. Bake in a preheated oven at 180°C for 15-20 minutes until crispy on top and golden brown.

Turn the muffin tray upside down to remove the cakes.

sweets

At Zarbo we've proved beyond a doubt that most people have a sweet tooth, and our sweet items are among the most requested. Customers will recognize popular favourites, such as the Sticky Buns and the Zucchini Slice, but will also find new inspiration in this collection of mouthwatering delights.

In this selection of recipes I have tempered the comfort of sugar with the subtle silkiness of cream (the Pannacotta, p.92), tart and tangy citrus and spice (Saffron and Kaffir Lime Custard Tart, p.100), dense, rich texture (Crumbly Pistachio and Lime Cake, p.108) and Oriental perfumes (Figs with Orange Blossom Syrup, Sumac and Mascarpone, p.106).

Some of the recipes rediscover ingredients that were standard in our grandmothers' kitchens, like quinces (Quince and Hazelnut Frangipane Tart, p.105) – it's surprising how many people have a 100-year-old quince in their back yard and never know what to do with the unpromising-looking fruit. The sherry trifle that our grandmothers made for Sunday dinner appears in a light, sophisticated metamorphosis, moistened with sparkling wine (Berry and Mascarpone Trifle, p.97) and the licorice straps that grandfather bought us for a treat feature in the stunning Licorice Lemon Yoghurt Mousse (p.89).

Desserts are not a big part of Asian cuisine, but I have included the classic Black Glutinous Rice Pudding with a Mango, Lime and Mint Salsa (p.90).

And chocolate-lovers are not left out – there are truffles and cookies and the gloriously simple yet divinely rich Mousse au Chocolat (p.104).

70 Per Cent Chocolate Ginger Cookies

Makes 12-15

These cookies should come with a health warning: 'Danger, these are addictive' or 'Do you need these on your thighs?'. . .

150 g 70 per cent chocolate
80 g butter
180 g soft brown sugar
1/2 teaspoon vanilla essence
1 egg
115 g flour
30 g Dutch cocoa
1 teaspoon baking soda
pinch of salt
100 g crystallised ginger

Melt the chocolate in a double boiler and allow to cool.

Beat together the butter and sugar until pale and creamy. Beat in the vanilla and the egg. Sift together the flour, cocoa, soda and salt and fold in, followed by the chocolate and ginger. Cover with plastic wrap and refrigerate for 1 hour.

Shape tablespoonfuls of the mixture into balls and place on a baking tray lined with baking paper, allowing space for spreading during cooking.

Bake in a preheated oven at 180°C for approximately 15-20 minutes. Remove from the tray and cool on a wire rack.

Coffee Legend

Coffee, a fundamental feature of Zarbo and worldwide café life, is thought to have originated in Ethiopia. The story goes that a farmer noticed his sheep became invigorated after eating the small red berries of a shrub that grew wild. The farmer tried the berries himself and realised the sheep were onto something good. He passed his discovery and some berries on to a local monk who decided the Devil was at work and hurled the berries on the fire to destroy them. The resulting aroma overpowered him. He rescued the berries from the fire and threw them into water . . . and the rest is history.

Gelato-stuffed Panettone

Serves 8

Panettone is a light, yeast-based fruit cake originating from Milan, containing raisins and candied citrus peel. It is traditionally served at Christmas and is readily available in New Zealand around this time. On Christmas Day I will often have panettone for breakfast with strawberries and a fine champagne. This is a variation that I make when I have a cake left over. Lightly frozen, it is ideal to serve as a summer dessert.

1 750 g panettone
3 flavours of gelato, 300-400 mls
  of each
4 tablespoons Limoncello (p.128)
  or Cointreau

Slice the top of the panettone and set aside. Hollow out the panettone, leaving the sides approximately 2 cm thick. Layer the gelato inside. This may have to be done in stages, putting the cake into the freezer to allow each layer of gelato to become firm before adding the next. Replace the top of the panettone and freeze.

Remove from the freezer and pour the Limoncello over the cake shell, refreeze. Serve sliced into wedges with fresh berries.

Variation: Layer the gelato with berries.

Licorice Lemon Yoghurt Mousse

Serves 12

Usually I make this in a loaf tin and serve it in slices, but to dress it up I put it into individual glasses. These flavours work well together and I consider this to be one of my all-time favourite desserts.

5 licorice straps
300 mls cream
5 egg yolks
1 cup caster sugar

1 cup Lemon Curd (p. 126)
^{1}/$_2$ cup plain yoghurt
^{1}/$_2$ cup whipped cream

Soften the licorice straps slightly in a microwave, then place in a double boiler with 300 mls cream. Slowly melt the licorice over a low heat.

Place the egg yolks and caster sugar in a bowl over a double boiler and beat until pale. Fold in the licorice mixture. Line a loaf tin with plastic wrap, pour in the mixture and freeze until firm.

When the licorice mixture is firm, mix the Lemon Curd, yoghurt and whipped cream together and pour over the top. Freeze for approximately 24 hours.

If making in a tin, before serving dip bottom of tin briefly in hot water, unmould the dessert and cut in slices.

Black Glutinous Rice Pudding with Mango, Lime and Mint Salsa

Serves 6

Do not confuse black glutinous rice with wild rice – they are quite different. Cooked desserts don't feature largely in Asian cuisine, but this is one of my favourites. The rice has a very nutty flavour which I think works well with the richness of the coconut milk and the sweetness of the palm sugar.

1½ cups coconut milk
4 kaffir lime leaves, bruised
6 cardamom pods
2 star anise
1 stalk lemongrass
1 cinnamon stick
rind of 3 lemons
2 tablespoons grated palm sugar

1 cup black glutinous rice, soaked for a minimum of 8 hours (preferably overnight) with the water changed several times
1 cup grated palm sugar
pinch of salt
2 tablespoons grated ginger

Place the coconut milk, lime leaves, cardamom, star anise, lemongrass, cinnamon, lemon rind and 2 tablespoons of palm sugar in a saucepan and bring to the boil. Reduce the heat and simmer for 15-20 minutes. Strain, reserve the liquid and leave to cool completely. It will thicken as it cools.

Drain the rice well and put into a saucepan, add the palm sugar, salt and ginger and stir well. Add 2 cups of water, bring to the boil, reduce the heat and simmer for 20-30 minutes until the rice is tender. Most of the water should be absorbed.

Note: Different batches of rice have quite different gluten levels, therefore it is necessary to keep your eye on the rice while it is cooking. Sometimes I have had to add more water, at other times I have had to strain it. Also note the 10-minute variance allowed for cooking time.

Combine the rice and coconut milk liquid. To serve, distribute the pudding into bowls and top with the Mango, Lime and Mint Salsa. If you like, spoon over extra coconut cream.

MANGO, LIME AND MINT SALSA

1 fresh mango, stone and skin removed (or 1 400 g tin mango pieces)
grated rind of 2 limes
juice of 1 lime
3 tablespoons finely chopped fresh mint

Finely dice the mango. If using tinned mango, drain well before dicing. Add the lime rind, juice and mint, stir well.

Pannacotta

Serves 4

Pannacotta (Italian for 'cooked cream') is a set, eggless custard. Amost anything can be used for flavouring; with this one I have used vanilla and cinnamon. Play around with this recipe but make sure the flavours you use are not too dominant, so as not to overpower the subtleness of the silky pannacotta.

250 mls milk
445 mls cream
2 vanilla beans
135 g sugar
2 cinnamon sticks
zest of 1 lemon

4 x 2 g gelatine leaves, soaked in
    1 cup water

Place the milk, cream, vanilla beans, sugar, cinnamon sticks and lemon zest into a pot and bring slowly to the boil. Stir occasionally. Once boiled, strain.

Strain the gelatine and add to the cream mix. When the gelatine has fully dissolved in the cream mix, strain again. Pour the mixture into a serving dish or mould and allow to set.

Note: If you want the dessert moulded, freeze the pannacotta in the mould, then dip the mould in warm water and turn out to serve.

Many recipes, both savoury and sweet, call for toasted spices or nuts. Toasting dry spices for a few minutes over a medium heat until they are fragrant releases an enzyme that enhances their flavour. I use my wok for this.

To toast nuts, spread the nuts evenly in one layer on a baking tray and toast in a 180°C preheated oven until lightly browned. Stir a few times, and keep your eye on them as they burn quickly. Remove from the tray as soon as they come out of the oven to prevent further cooking.

Zucchini Slice

Makes 24

This is one of the more unusual slices that we make at Zarbo, but its recipe is also one of the most requested.

BASE
125 g butter
¹/₂ cup sugar
¹/₂ egg
200 g flour

Beat the butter and sugar, add the egg then the flour, stir until combined. Press in a thin layer into a greased, lined 30 x 20 cm tray. Bake in a preheated oven at 180°C until golden brown, approximately 15 minutes.

TOPPING
5 eggs
3 cups brown sugar
1¹/₂ teaspoons vanilla essence
pinch of salt
3 tablespoons flour
100 g sliced almonds
2¹/₄ cups coconut thread
1 cup chocolate chips
2¹/₄ cups grated zucchini (grate just prior to mixing through)

Whisk the eggs, sugar, vanilla and salt until combined. Mix in the flour, almonds, coconut and chocolate. Grate the zucchini and mix in.

Spread the topping mixture evenly over the prepared base. Bake in a preheated oven at 180°C for approximately 30-45 minutes.

The cooking time will vary depending on the amount of moisture in the zucchini, and individual ovens. The slice should be firm but soft.

Berry and Mascarpone Trifle

Serves 8

Trifle is a classic English dessert. This is a contemporary version in which I have replaced the sponge with savoiardi fingers and the sherry with Prosecco, an Italian sparkling wine.

100 g icing sugar
1100 g mascarpone
1 cup cream
400 mls Prosecco (or other dry sparkling wine)
300 g savoiardi (ladies' fingers)
1 cup blackberries
1 cup raspberries
2 cups strawberries (optional)

Sift the icing sugar onto the mascarpone, fold in gently, being careful not to overmix which would cause the mascarpone to split. Mix in the cream.

Soak enough savoiardi fingers in the Prosecco to cover the base of the dish (don't oversoak or they will turn to mush).

Place a layer of mascarpone mix on top of the savoiardi, then a handful of berries. Repeat this twice, making sure enough berries are left to cover the top of the trifle.

Truffles

Each recipe makes approximately 16

Here are truffles to suit various degrees of sweet-toothed sophistication. Save the children's recipe for a rainy day in the school holidays. Savour the others with coffee at any time.

FRUIT AND NUT TRUFFLES
100 g dried peaches
100 g dried Turkish figs
100 g candied orange peel
1/2 cup coarsely chopped pistachios
1 cup coconut flakes
1 cup crumbled wine biscuits
3/4 cup sweetened condensed milk

Chop the peaches, figs and peel into small pieces. In a medium-size bowl mix together the fruit and pistachios, coconut flakes, biscuit crumbs and condensed milk. Roll into 20 mm balls and refrigerate until firm.

Variation: Roll the balls in extra coconut flakes and melted white chocolate before refrigerating.

CHOCOLATE TRUFFLES
70 g glacé cherries
70 g crystallised angelica (available from specialty food stores)
70 g crystallised ginger
1 1/2 cups toasted ground hazelnuts
120 g dark chocolate buttons
2 teaspoons Dutch cocoa
2 tablespoons sweetened condensed milk

Chop the cherries, angelica and ginger into small pieces. Add the toasted ground hazelnuts. Heat the chocolate buttons until slightly melted and add. Add the sieved cocoa and condensed milk. Mix until well combined. Roll into 20 mm balls and refrigerate until firm.

Variation: Roll the balls in a mix of toasted chopped hazelnuts and melted chocolate before refrigerating.

CHILDREN'S TRUFFLES
90 g jelly babies
60 g marshmallows
70 g milk chocolate buttons
70 g white chocolate buttons
50 g coconut chips
1 1/2 cups crumbed wine biscuits
210 g condensed milk

Roughly chop the jelly babies, marshmallows, milk and white chocolate buttons, and set aside. Mix together the coconut chips, biscuit crumbs and condensed milk. Add the jelly babies mix and combine well. Roll into 20 mm balls and refrigerate until firm.

Saffron and Kaffir Lime Custard Tart

Serves 8-10

Custard tarts are always popular. I have developed this one as an alternative to the traditional and sometimes overly sweet version. Saffron gives the tart a rich, earthy flavour and the citrus of the lime leaves cuts the sweetness.

1 recipe Sweet Short Pastry, baked blind (see p.127) in a 26 cm tin

375 mls full-cream milk
375 mls cream
grated rind of 1¹/₂ limes
3 good-size pinches saffron
dash of vanilla essence

3 large eggs
3 extra egg yolks
90 g caster sugar

6 kaffir lime leaves, very finely shredded

Heat the milk, cream, lime rind, saffron and vanilla in a saucepan until nearly boiling.

In a bowl beat the eggs, yolks and sugar until creamy.

Add the lime leaves to the milk/cream mixture. Pour into the egg mix and combine. Pour into the prepared base.

Bake in a preheated oven at 160ºC for approximately 40 minutes.

Sweet Lavosh

Makes 20 triangles

Lavosh is traditionally a light savoury crispbread served with dips or as a sandwich. It is also known as Armenian cracker bread. This sweet version is excellent to serve with Pannacotta (p.92) or simply with some fresh berries and mascarpone.

40 g butter
300 g flour
pinch salt
5 g icing sugar
1 large egg
85 mls milk
extra icing sugar for topping

Rub the butter into the dry ingredients, add the egg and milk, mix until the dough comes away from the sides of the bowl. Rest the dough for 30 minutes at room temperature.

Roll the dough into a sheet 2 mm thick and cut into triangles. Place the triangles on a greased or lined baking tray, brush with milk and sprinkle with extra icing sugar.

Bake in a preheated oven at 180°C for 15 minutes. When cold, coat with icing sugar.

Mousse au Chocolat

Serves 4 (note that larger portions are shown in the photo; for servings this size, double the recipe)

This is a recipe supplied by my former head baker, Sally Ann, now working in Belgium. When we think of Belgium we immediately think of chocolate. I like this mousse because it is much lighter than some of the other rich ones I have made over the years, in spite of the fact that 70 per cent chocolate is used.

50 g 70 per cent dark Belgian
   chocolate
3 dessertspoons milk
200 mls cream
50 g icing sugar
3 egg whites
chocolates for decoration

Melt the chocolate with the milk in a double boiler, cool slightly. Whip the cream with the sugar. Whisk the egg whites till firm. Firstly fold the chocolate into the cream then carefully add the stiffened whites, bit by bit until combined.

Spoon into glasses, top with chocolate decorations, refrigerate for at least 1 hour.

Quince and Hazelnut Frangipane Tart

Serves 8-10

Quinces have been around for over 4000 years. Ancient Romans used them extensively in their cuisine, and when a quince was given to one's lover it was considered a symbol of commitment.

1 recipe Sweet Short Pastry, baked blind (see p.127) in a 26 cm flan tin

200 g butter
200 g sugar
4 eggs
250 g ground hazelnuts
4 large quinces, peeled, cored and sliced finely

GLAZE
3 tablespoons apricot jam
2 tablespoons water

Cream the butter and sugar, add eggs one at a time, mixing thoroughly after each is added. Fold in the ground hazelnuts. Spread frangipane mix into the prepared pastry case. Arrange the quince slices on the top.

Bake in a preheated oven at 170°C for 30-40 minutes. If the tart browns too quickly, decrease temperature for the remainder of the cooking time.

To glaze: boil together the apricot jam and water. Brush the glaze over the tart when it is cooked.

Figs with Orange Blossom Syrup, Sumac and Mascarpone

Serves 4

This is so simple and the flavours work so well together. Figs originate from Southern Europe. They were held sacred by the Romans and were considered a symbol of peace and prosperity. Many of the hundreds of varieties of figs grow well in New Zealand. The highly perfumed flavour of orange blossom water comes from the distillation of bitter-orange blossoms. Sumac, a crushed red berry native to the Middle East, has a fruity citrus flavour.

600 g caster sugar
300 mls water
100 mls orange blossom water
16 fresh figs, cut in half
pinch sumac
4 tablespoons mascarpone

Place the sugar, water and orange blossom water in a heavy-based saucepan and bring to the boil, reduce the heat and simmer for 10 minutes.

Put the fig halves on a baking tray, grill for 2-3 minutes until lightly browned. Place the fig halves on serving plates, pour over the syrup, sprinkle with a little sumac and serve with a dollop of mascarpone.

Crumbly Pistachio and Lime Cake

Serves 12-16

Polenta gives this traditional Florentine cake a dense texture, while pistachios and lime intensify the flavour. Try it with a glass of grappa or a strong coffee.

125 g pistachio nuts
1/2 cup fine polenta
1/2 cup caster sugar
1 cup flour
zest of 3 limes
120 g softened butter
2 egg yolks
icing sugar to dust

Lightly toast the pistachios and allow to cool. Remove their husks. Cool completely and place in a food processor and process. Add the polenta, sugar and flour and blend. Then add the lime zest, half the butter and 1 egg yolk and blend. Add the rest of the butter and egg and blend until well mixed and crumbly.

Line the base of a 23 cm baking tin with baking paper, lightly butter or spray. Press the mix into the tin. Lightly dust with extra sugar.

Bake in a preheated oven at 180°C for 35-40 minutes.

Remove from the tin, allow to cool slightly and cut into small wedges while still warm. Dust with icing sugar.

Stone Fruit Crumble

Serves 6-8

Crumbles are another favourite British dessert that I think should make a return. Any fruit or berry can be used in these. Here I have used plums and nectarines, available in early autumn when evenings are starting to turn crisp and a warm dessert is an appealing idea. Rolled oats and sliced almonds in the crumble mix give extra crunch and flavour.

CRUMBLE
350 g butter
2 tablespoons honey
1 cup self-raising flour
1 1/2 teaspoons cinnamon
1 cup brown sugar
1/2 cup coconut thread
1 1/2 cups rolled oats
1/2 cup sliced almonds

Melt the butter and honey together. Sieve in the flour, add the other ingredients, combine and set aside.

SYRUP
1 kg sugar
500 mls water
1 cinnamon stick
1 vanilla bean
zest of 1 lemon

1.5 kg plums
1.5 kg nectarines

Place the syrup ingredients in a pot and bring to the boil. Remove the stones from the fruit, peel and slice, add to the syrup and simmer until just tender. Drain well, reserving 1/2 cup syrup. Place the fruit in a baking dish, pour over the reserved syrup and top with the crumble mix. Bake in a preheated oven at 170ºC for 30-40 minutes until golden brown.

Sticky Buns

Makes 8

Sticky buns are a resounding Zarbo favourite, and one of the most requested recipes. We usually bake these only on Saturdays when there is a regular crowd lining up for them.

1 sheet Danish pastry
3 tablespoons apricot jam
1/2 cup walnuts
1/2 cup sultanas
1/2 teaspoon ground cinnamon
50 g butter
1/2 cup brown sugar

2 cups Caramel Sauce
1/2 cup pistachios, roughly chopped

Place the Danish pastry sheet on a lightly floured bench. Spread the apricot jam evenly over the pastry. Scatter the walnuts, sultanas and cinnamon evenly over the jam. Roll up, and slice into 8 even-sized rolls.

Spray 8 muffin moulds with baking spray. Evenly distribute the butter in the bases of the moulds, then even amounts of the brown sugar. Place a roll into each of the moulds. Leave in a warm place until the rolls have doubled in size.

In a preheated oven, bake at 180°C for 15-20 minutes or until golden brown. Turn the rolls out of the moulds while warm to prevent them setting and sticking. Pour over the Caramel Sauce and scatter the pistachios on top.

CARAMEL SAUCE
150 g sugar
75 mls water
375 mls cream

Place the sugar and water in a pan, bring to the boil and cook to a golden brown colour, then cool the base of the pan in cold water. Pour the cream into the caramel, bring slowly to the boil, and mix. Allow to cool before using.

basics

This section is partly about fundamental and versatile food components that are good to have on hand or which you can make almost 'by heart' when you need them for other dishes. It's also about technique – once you've mastered the making of a basic mayonnaise, for example, the most exotic variation will be a breeze.

everal of the recipes from the first Zarbo book are so essential to my own basics list that they re-appear here too.

I have included sauces and dressings that, although elementary, will turn ordinary ingredients like pasta or salad vegetables into interesting dishes. The Tomato Sauce (p.117) is a classic in its own right, but you can add your own touches. Asian-inspired sauces like the Wasabi Dressing (p.122) can be used for dipping or to bring a salad to life. These sauces are easy to make and can be kept in the fridge for several days.

The ancient and satisfying art of bread making is demystified in the simple recipe for Pizza Base (p.121). You can add traditional toppings or invent your own. Another extremely useful baking technique – blind baking of pastry cases – is explained on p.127.

So – usefulness and versatility is the theme of this section . . . and it even includes a basic luxury, the Limoncello (p.128), an Italian liqueur, simply made with fresh lemons, that you can enjoy on its own or use to take an everyday dessert to new heights.

Basic Tomato Sauce

Makes 2$^1/_2$-3 cups

This very traditional recipe comes from early Neapolitan pizza makers. Feel free to add your own personal touches to the sauce, but don't be tempted to leave out the anchovies – the secret of its success. Store it in the fridge for up to 1 week. Use it on pastas and pizza.

4 cloves garlic, finely chopped
4 tablespoons extra virgin olive oil
4 anchovy fillets
2 x 400 g tins whole peeled Italian tomatoes
$^1/_2$ teaspoon dried oregano
$^1/_2$ cup dry white wine
salt and pepper

Sauté the garlic in the oil. Add the anchovies, sauté and break up into a paste. Add the tomatoes (crush them by hand to give the desired texture), dried oregano and wine.

Simmer uncovered for approximately 20-30 minutes to reduce to a thick sauce. Add salt and pepper to taste.

Measuring Spoons and Scales

While a certain intuitive 'feel' for food is indispensable to inspirational cooking, it is important in baking recipes to measure things accurately. A reliable set of measuring spoons and scales are kitchen essentials.

Mayonnaise/Aioli

Makes 1-1½ cups

I've included several mayonnaise/aioli recipes here. Extremely versatile, these are always useful to have on hand as a dip on platters, with bread, as a sauce on sandwiches, to accompany quiches and cold meats or to toss through salads. Mayonnaise is a standard thick dressing made by combining egg yolk, oil and lemon juice or vinegar. Aioli, which originated in Provence, is basic mayonnaise flavoured with garlic. Once you have mastered the basic technique these are very simple to make at home using a food processor. They will keep, refrigerated, for 4-5 days.

BASIC MAYONNAISE
3 egg yolks
juice of ½ lemon
salt and pepper to taste
1 cup olive oil

Place the egg yolk, lemon juice, salt and pepper into a food processor and whizz to combine. Take the lid off and with a spatula scrape down the sides and around the base of the bowl, replace the lid and whizz again.

Add a few drops of the oil, whizz to fully incorporate, repeat a few times until the sauce is smoothly blended and thickened. Then with the machine running, gradually pour in the rest of the oil in a very thin stream. If your processor has an attachment to drip-feed the oil, use it. If the oil is poured in too quickly the sauce will split.

AIOLI

Make as for Basic Mayonnaise, but add 2 cloves finely crushed garlic (or to taste) with the egg yolk, lemon juice and salt and pepper.

DILL AND CITRUS AIOLI

Makes 2 cups

The dill and lemon in this aioli makes it especially suited to serving with seafood. Try it with your favourite grilled fish or the Salmon Filo on p.70.

1 clove garlic, crushed
2 tablespoons fresh dill
2 tablespoons capers
zest of 1 lemon
salt and pepper
1½ cups extra virgin olive oil

Combine the garlic, dill, capers, lemon zest, salt and pepper in a food processor. Very slowly add the olive oil as per Basic Mayonnaise instructions.

ROASTED GARLIC AND SAFFRON AIOLI

Makes 1½ cups

The intense flavours produced by roasting the garlic and the earthiness of the saffron make this beautifully creamy aioli ideally suited to serving with fresh vegetables. Try it also spread on rounds of French bread and lightly grilled.

3 egg yolks
2 heads of garlic, roasted (adjust quantity to personal taste)
1 teaspoon saffron thread, infused by heating with the juice of 1 lemon in a microwave for about 20 seconds and allowed to cool completely
salt and pepper
1½ cups of extra virgin olive oil

Combine the egg yolks, garlic, saffron infusion, salt and pepper in a food processor. Very slowly pour in the oil as per Basic Mayonnaise instructions to form a creamy texture.

Traditional Pizza

Makes 10 individual pizzas

Individual pizzas are fantastic for a light lunch or as a casual entrée. I personally favour a traditional rustic Neapolitan pizza, with a thin and crisp base. Toppings should be kept traditional and simple. (Adding ingredients such as bananas or tandoori meat is a capital offence in my opinion!) The Basic Tomato Sauce (p.117) is always a good start and anchovies, oven-baked tomatoes, mozzarella, olives, capers and garlic are essentials.

15 g dried yeast
6 tablespoons lukewarm water
3 tablespoons 00 Italian (or plain) flour

2¹/₂ cups 00 Italian (or plain) flour
pinch of salt
approximately ³/₄ cup extra lukewarm water

Combine the yeast, water and 3 tablespoons flour to form a 'soup'. Cover with a damp towel and put aside in a warm, draught-free place for approximately 30 minutes until it has expanded.

Place the remaining flour and salt into a bowl and add the 'soup'. Knead for approximately 10 minutes, adding extra water until a well combined ball has been formed. Cover with the towel and place back in the warm, draught-free place for approximately another 30 minutes until the ball has doubled in size. Remove the dough to a floured work surface and 'break down'.

At this stage, decide how you want to serve the pizza and roll the dough to the required sizes and thickness. Add the toppings. Cook individual pizzas in a preheated oven at 220ºC for 7-10 minutes until crisp and golden.

To Freeze Pizza Bases
Form the dough into balls each of sufficient quantity for 1 pizza base. Place in individual freezer bags. The dough will need to be thawed completely before using.

Asian Vinaigrette

Makes 1-1½ cups

Keep a jar of this dressing on hand (store in the fridge for up to 10 days) to have over salad greens, or try with a Thai beef salad.

1 clove garlic, diced
2 kaffir lime leaves, finely shredded
salt and pepper
50 mls sesame oil
juice of 1 lime
75 mls rice wine vinegar
1 tablespoon grated palm sugar
1 tablespoon Thai basil (if unavailable use regular basil)

Combine all ingredients.

Wasabi Dressing

Makes 1 cup

Give salads a new dimension with this dressing or use as a dipping sauce with sushi or spring rolls.

juice of 2 lemons
3 teaspoons wasabi powder
100 mls sesame oil
2 teaspoons finely diced ginger
2 cloves garlic, crushed
100 mls Kikkoman soy sauce

Combine all ingredients.

Marinades

Marinades are designed for soaking meats, poultry, fish or vegetables so that they absorb flavour. The acid in a marinade, such as vinegar or lemon juice, helps to tenderise tougher cuts of meat. I usually marinate meats and chicken in a plastic bag, and fish or vegetables in a bowl. How long to marinate depends on the size of the pieces and how readily they absorb the marinade (meat takes longer than fish or vegetables). Drain the marinade before cooking.

ASIAN MARINADE

juice of 1 lemon
2 tablespoons fish sauce
2 tablespoons sesame oil
1 clove garlic, finely crushed
salt and pepper to taste

Combine all ingredients. Use on lamb or duck.

MEDITERRANEAN MARINADE

1 teaspoon finely chopped fresh rosemary
1 clove garlic, crushed
6 tablespoons olive oil
6 tablespoons raspberry vinegar
salt and pepper to taste

Combine all ingredients. Use for fish, lamb or mushrooms.

MIDDLE EASTERN/NORTH AFRICAN MARINADE

1 tablespoon Spanish smoked paprika
juice of 2 lemons
1 clove garlic, crushed
2 teaspoons ground coriander
salt and pepper to taste

Combine all ingredients. Use on vegetables, fish and pork.

Asian Ingredients

The list given here is by no means comprehensive. It is simply to familiarise you with some of the Asian ingredients used in this book – and, I hope, encourage you to explore, discover and experiment.

ASIAN GREENS

Get past bok choy! Choose a selection from the variety available at Asian stores, such as gai choy (large green leaf with a mustard flavour) or choy sum (a yellow-flowering Chinese cabbage). You will be surprised at some of the flavours and how easy they are to prepare. Use your own combination in the Asian Green Stir-fry (p.46).

CHINESE SWEETENED RICE VINEGAR

Flavoured with palm sugar and star anise, this vinegar has the most amazing rounded, sweet/tart balance. I use it in marinades, as in the Barbecued Chicken Skewers (p.18) and also in sauces and dressings.

FISH SAUCE

This pungent sauce made from air-dried salted fish is essential in Vietnamese and Thai cooking. I use it in everything from marinades (p.123) to dipping sauces as in the traditional Vietnamese Nuoc Cham (p.72) to serve with barbecued fish.

GARLIC AND GINGER

Although you will be very familiar with these, you may not have discovered what a difference it makes to use the freshest available product – precrushed just doesn't do it. Garlic should always be firm, with a tight papery skin. At different times of the year fresh young ginger is available, crisp and juicy with almost transparent skin. I julienne this and use it in dishes such as the Crispy Vermicelli Noodles (p.55). At other times of year I add ginger to casseroles, stir-fries and soups.

KAFFIR LIME LEAVES

The intense fresh flavour of these unusual double leaves is unbeatable. Use the whole leaf to flavour soups or in rice dishes, or shred the leaves and add to marinades and sauces. The leaves are available in dried form or fresh from specialty fruit and vegetable stores. Fresh leaves can be frozen. Plants are also available – be careful, they have long vicious thorns.

KECAP MANIS

The sweetness of this thick, black, syrupy traditional Indonesian soy sauce comes from the addition of palm sugar. I use it in dressings and marinades, especially for barbecue marinades because it caramelises as it cooks.

MIRIN

A mild-flavoured Japanese cooking condiment used in marinades and dressings.

PALM SUGAR

This is the concentrated sap of the palm tree, boiled then poured into moulds to set. When I first used palm sugar its richness reminded me of Russian fudge. Use it in sauces, marinades and desserts such as the Black Glutinous Rice Pudding on (p.90).

SZECHWAN PEPPERCORNS

These are in fact not a peppercorn but a mildly hot spiced berry from a shrub native to China. Add these to your pepper grinder or try a 50/50 mix with sea salt; dry roast and grind in a mortar and pestle. Use as a seasoning over grilled chicken, pork or fish. I have used this spice in the Asian Spoons with Minted Sweet Chilli Duck (p.21).

TAMARIND

The fruit of a tree native to Asia and India, usually available in block form. It has a sour flavour essential in many Asian dishes and is often used as an alternative to lemon and lime juice. Try it out in the Pumpkin, Tamarind and Kumara Curry (p.76).

STAR ANISE

A beautiful, mysterious spice, from a variety of magnolia native to China. Its strong licorice flavour should be only hinted at in dishes, used to scent rather than flavour. It lends itself to baking, dressings, main meals (both Asian and North African) and desserts – I have used it in the Black Glutinous Rice Pudding (p.90). It is also an essential spice in the ras el-hanout used with the Moroccan Lamb Shanks (p.67)

Lemon Curd

Makes approximately 600 g

Use this curd as a spread (great on toasted bagels), as a tart filling, and in the Licorice Lemon Yoghurt Mousse (p.89). It will keep in the fridge for up to 2 weeks.

300 g sugar
200 g butter, diced
3 organic lemons, grated rind and juice
3 eggs, whisked

Place the sugar and diced butter in a heatproof bowl and place over a saucepan of simmering water. Do not let the bowl touch the water. Stir until the butter is melted and the sugar dissolved. Remove the bowl from the heat and allow to cool a bit, then mix in the lemon juice and rind.

When the mixture is just warm (if it is too hot it will scramble the eggs), stir in the whisked eggs. Place back over the saucepan of simmering water and stir constantly until the curd starts to thicken, but not curdle, approximately 10-15 minutes.

Sweet Short Pastry

Makes one 28 cm tart

This pastry is excellent for the many sweet tart recipes that require precooked cases, such as the Saffron and Kaffir Lime Custard Tart (p.100) or Quince and Hazelnut Frangipane Tart (p.105). The blind baking technique described here can be used for all short pastry cases.

200 g butter, softened
150 g icing sugar
2 eggs
400 g plain flour, sifted

Cream the butter and icing sugar together. Beat in the eggs one at a time. Mix in the flour. Remove from the processor or bowl and knead until well combined. Pat the dough into a ball, wrap in plastic wrap and refrigerate for 30 minutes before using.

Variation: For chocolate sweet pastry replace 75 g of flour with Dutch cocoa.

To Blind Bake

Roll out the pastry on a floured board, place in a tin of selected size for the recipe being used. Cover the pastry with tinfoil or baking paper, pressing it into the sides. Cover with baking beans and bake in a preheated oven at 180°C for 6-8 minutes.

Remove the beans and tinfoil or paper, prick the pastry with a fork and brush the surface with beaten egg white. Return to the oven for a further 4-5 minutes. This will seal the pastry and ensure its crispness.

Limoncello

Makes approximately 750 mls

Limoncello is a traditional lemon liqueur originating from the Amalfi Coast of Italy. It is simple enough to make at home – the biggest problem is sourcing the correct lemons. The lemons in the Italian markets are the size of a baseball, but New Zealand-grown Meyer lemons are fine for this recipe. Keep Limoncello in the freezer and serve after dinner, a nip in a glass of champagne, over strawberries or in the Gelato-stuffed Panettone (p.88).

6 lemons
3 cups vodka
3 cups caster sugar
2 cups water

Soak the lemons in cold water for 1 hour, remove and dry well. Very finely peel the lemons, ensuring no pith is attached. Put the peel in a large jar and top with 2 cups of vodka. Cover and allow to stand in a cool dark place for 3 days.

In a pot combine the sugar and 2 cups of water, bring to the boil, reduce the heat and simmer for 20 minutes. Allow to cool completely. Add the syrup to the vodka/peel mix and combine well. Allow to stand in a cool dark place for 2 days.

Add the remaining vodka, cork and stand in a cool dark place for 2 more days.

Filter through muslin, returning the liquid to the bottle. Stand for 1 week before using.

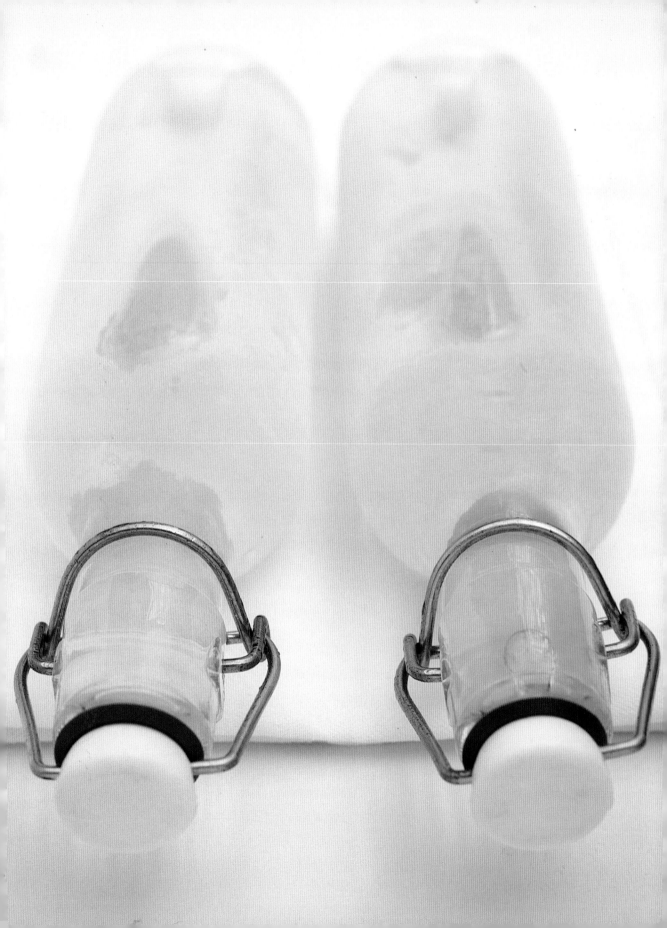

index